CREATED BY BRITTANY BACINSKI

YOUR DAILY VIBE

DAILY ENERGY JOURNAL

All Good Juju

www.brittanybacinski.com

"Heal the world with what heals you."

BRITTANY BACINSKI

introduction

I'm Brittany Bacinski, Acclaimed Cookbook Author of the cookbook series Hippie Eats, Host of the All Good Juju Podcast, Spiritual Intuitive, Mama, Writer and Wellness Enthusiast. I have my hands in many pots and have become a master of many things. I never used to be this way. I never used to follow my bliss or do these things that lit me up.

I've always been a dreamer, but I wasn't always a do-er. I used to live a life that felt anything but authentic and in constant fear of failure. I'd color safely in the lines, do what I was told and what was expected of me. Life was pretty uneventful then until I had my great awakening, literally after waking up from a dream of the word, "Law of Attraction."

I thought maybe it was a movie or a show on TV, so I googled it. My life was changed forever after.

The Law of Attraction is the attractive, magnetic power of the universe that manifests through everyone and through everything. "What you think, you become," also explains it simply. This law attracts thoughts, ideas, people, situations, circumstances, and the things you think about.

Since then, energy has become a huge part of my life. I've left behind my old ways that weren't serving me to finally striking the healthiest, most energetically aligned balanced life.

I took a social media detox and focused on quieting the noise around me so I could fully absorb the guided information from the universe. After mediating one night, I clearly heard my soul tell me to, "Heal the world through what heals you."

When I think about what healed me, it comes down to a combination of practices that led to where I'm at today. A daily journal practice, mindful present living, consuming high vibrational foods and beverages, moving my body to shake up my energy and manifesting my dreams with a soulfully aligned mindset.

The Hippie Eats Cookbooks were born out of sharing with the world what healed me first: My relationship with food. The cookbooks include delicious high-vibrational meals that helped me heal my body. Before I changed what I consumed, I was sick with horrible inflammatory bowel issues and chronic anxiety. Fed up almost 10 years ago, I began to truly nourish my body while healing my mind, body and spirit. And I haven't looked back.

If you're ready to take control of your life, own your daily vibration, hold yourself accountable for your energy and finally shift from a dreamer to a do-er, the Daily Vibe Energy Journal is for you.

I can't wait to see what's next for you. Connect with me on Instagram @brittanybacinski and use hashtag #dailyvibejournal to share your beautiful journal in high vibe places and help spread this good vibe movement with the rest of the world.

Peace, love, & good vibes,

Brittany Bacinski

low vibrations

All living things have vibrations. Your vibration is your energetic frequency. Having a low vibration is connected to lowered energy and negative, oppressive emotions. How can you tell if you suffer from a low vibration?

Below are common feelings you can expect with a low vibration:

* Uneasiness
* Anger
* Jealousy
* Bitterness
* Pessimism
* Guilt
* Blame
* Restlessness

Things that lower your vibration:

1. Junk food and fast food
2. Dehydration
3. Toxic overload
4. Stressing overly on the past or future too much
5. Constant digital overload
6. Drugs and alcohol
7. Lack of movement
8. Lack of sleep

high vibrations

High vibrations are linked to positivity, happiness, love, compassion, higher energy levels and peacefulness.

Things that raise your vibration include:

1. Living plant-based foods from the earth (fresh fruits and vegetables)
2. Water (Filtered is best)
3. Non-toxic products
4. Living in the present moment
5. Frequent unplugging from digital devices
6. Abstaining from drugs and alcohol
7. Moving your body and energy
8. Good rest
9. Journaling and a grateful heart
10. Breath work and meditation
11. Distancing from low vibrational people or situations
12. Spending time in your creative magic

gratitude practice

Have you ever noticed that one positive thought in the morning can change your whole day? And the reverse is also true. One negative thought can make your whole day a wreck.

The benefits of practicing gratitude are nearly endless. People who regularly practice gratitude by taking time to notice and reflect upon the things they're thankful for experience more positive emotions, feel more alive, sleep better, express more compassion and kindness, and even have stronger immune systems.

A grateful heart is a magnet for miracles. A regular gratitude practice may cause miracles. Yes, you read that right.

I've been journaling gratitude over the last 5 years and since then I can tell you as living proof that I've manifested more in my life simply being grateful (each and everyday) and by showing God (the universe, spirit, source energy, who/whatever you believe in) that I was grateful through my journaling practice.

I grew up low income in a single wide trailer with all odd stacked against me. And here I am, mother to two beautiful boys living in my dream house, a 5x published author, creator and do-er of my wildest dreams. I became debt-free by 26, paying off thousands of dollars in student loans with this practice and have watched everything I've journaled come true. This will change your life.

*"if this isn't nice,
i don't know what is."-
Kurt Vonnegut*

Look out of your window and say it.
Smile at yourself in the mirror and say
it. Hug your kid or partner or friend
tightly and say it.

Take a bite of your favorite meal and
say it. When your feet hit the floor in
the morning, say it. Say this quote
every single day. And watch how much
happier you become.

creative magic

Stressed? Moody? Snappy? Anxious or deflated? Ask yourself this: Have you spent time in creativity lately? I've noticed that I'm not at my best when I haven't spent time in my creative magic.

Do one thing creative each day and see the difference in your mood and vibe for yourself. It could be anything from doodling, writing, painting, gardening, baking, interior decor, organizing, building something, making a vision board or whatever feels like creativity to you. Try it and watch your magic unfold daily.

movement

After my second baby, I've realized that it's hard getting the strength to move your body, it's even harder to leave the baby to exercise. But if you're able to, moving your body will shift your mind to a better place.

It's not just about the physical change of fitness or "bouncing back" into those pre-baby jeans or getting down to your high school weight.

I realized that I manifest more out of life (at a much faster speed) when I prioritize fitness in some way. It helps me strengthen my mind, which is now so important as a mom.

I feel stronger mentally when I move my body.

Everyone I look up to—from CEO's to authors of quirky literary fiction novels, they all have one thing in common. They all make fitness a priority in one way or another. It's not just for looks. They understand the magic behind fitness as a spiritual practice. They have learned that feeling good is the key to living an abundant life.

So here I am with you. Changing my mindset. Moving my body and making it a priority. Viewing fitness as a spiritual practice. And it doesn't hurt that I'm also gaining the physical strength to zoom matchbox cars with my boys or chase them on their bikes before they fall off.

Movement is medicine.

Great ways to shake up your energy and move your body include yoga, dancing in your kitchen, twerking in your pj's, weightlifting, running, resistance training, cardio, whatever it is that you do and enjoy, make it a part of your spiritual practice.

When the endorphins kick in, start imagining your higher self. Visualize your success as you're moving and breathing faster. This, my friends, is the secret sauce. You want a better vibe or an abundant life at a rapid speed? Shake your energy up!

your energy report

What is your intutition telling you? If you pull tarot, oracle or affirmation cards, or even read daily scripture or devotional from the Bible, this is where the space where you'd journal what you came across for the day and what messages you felt were for you.This is an excellent way to connect with your own intuition and soul's guidance.

If you don't have those tools in your practice, try noticing signs from above. Was there a cardinal outside of your window this morning? Did you wake up from a dream that felt like it had a deeper meaning to you? Did something feel like a sign today? Any overall vibe and feelings you may have this day, try writing them down here. You'll be surprised with what the universe is trying to tell you.

your highest self

Think of the best version of yourself and who you want to be. What does this person look like. What clothes are you wearing, what foods are you eating? What healthy habits do you have as your best self? What goals and dreams have you accomplished? Nothing is too big or off limits. This is your higher self. The person who has reached the top of the mountain. The real you. The higher self is the you that is unlimited in potential and fully conscious. Start seeing yourself as you truly are. What you seek is seeking you. Show up as this person and everything you've ever wanted is yours.

In this next section, I want you to write a letter to your higher self. Tell yourself thank you for all your dreams that came true. Be as detailed as possible and be clear in your vision. Someday you'll look back at it and be blown away.

dear highest self,

love always & forever,

MY
DAILY
VIBE

Vibe I feel right now:

Vibe I want to feel:

5 things I am grateful for:

    1.

    2.

    3.

    4.

    5.

Draw your mood:

Low Vibe Checklist:

☐ Low Water Intake   ☐ Alcohol   ☐ Negative Energy

☐ Poor Sleep Quality   ☐ Toxic Overload   ☐ Digital Device Overload

☐ Lack of Movement   ☐ Low Vibe Foods   ☐ Other/ Explain

High Vibe Checklist:

☐ Well Hydrated   ☐ No Alcohol   ☐ Positive Energy

☐ Great Sleep Quality   ☐ Low Toxic Input   ☐ Digital Device Balance

☐ Movement   ☐ High Vibe Foods   ☐ Other/Explain

I will use my creative magic by:

I will move my energy by:

Energy report:

Note from my higher self:

MY DAILY VIBE

Vibe I feel right now:

Vibe I want to feel:

5 things I am grateful for:

1.

2.

3.

4.

5.

Draw your mood:

Low Vibe Checklist:

☐ Low Water Intake ☐ Alcohol ☐ Negative Energy

☐ Poor Sleep Quality ☐ Toxic Overload ☐ Digital Device Overload

☐ Lack of Movement ☐ Low Vibe Foods ☐ Other/ Explain

High Vibe Checklist:

- [ ] Well Hydrated
- [ ] No Alcohol
- [ ] Positive Energy
- [ ] Great Sleep Quality
- [ ] Low Toxic Input
- [ ] Digital Device Balance
- [ ] Movement
- [ ] High Vibe Foods
- [ ] Other/Explain

I will use my creative magic by:

I will move my energy by:

Energy report:

Note from my higher self:

MY
DAILY
VIBE

Vibe I feel right now:

Vibe I want to feel:

5 things I am grateful for:

    1.

    2.

    3.

    4.

    5.

Draw your mood:

Low Vibe Checklist:

☐	Low Water Intake	☐	Alcohol	☐	Negative Energy
☐	Poor Sleep Quality	☐	Toxic Overload	☐	Digital Device Overload
☐	Lack of Movement	☐	Low Vibe Foods	☐	Other/ Explain

High Vibe Checklist:

☐ Well Hydrated   ☐ No Alcohol   ☐ Positive Energy

☐ Great Sleep Quality   ☐ Low Toxic Input   ☐ Digital Device Balance

☐ Movement   ☐ High Vibe Foods   ☐ Other/Explain

I will use my creative magic by:

I will move my energy by:

Energy report:

Note from my higher self:

MY
DAILY
VIBE

Vibe I feel right now:

Vibe I want to feel:

5 things I am grateful for:

    1.

    2.

    3.

    4.

    5.

Draw your mood:

Low Vibe Checklist:

☐ Low Water Intake   ☐ Alcohol   ☐ Negative Energy

☐ Poor Sleep Quality   ☐ Toxic Overload   ☐ Digital Device Overload

☐ Lack of Movement   ☐ Low Vibe Foods   ☐ Other/ Explain

High Vibe Checklist:

☐ Well
Hydrated

☐ No
Alcohol

☐ Positive
Energy

☐ Great Sleep
Quality

☐ Low Toxic
Input

☐ Digital Device
Balance

☐ Movement

☐ High Vibe
Foods

☐ Other/Explain

I will use my creative magic by:

I will move my energy by:

Energy report:

Note from my higher self:

MY
DAILY
VIBE

Vibe I feel right now:

Vibe I want to feel:

5 things I am grateful for:

1.

2.

3.

4.

5.

Draw your mood:

Low Vibe Checklist:

☐ Low Water Intake   ☐ Alcohol   ☐ Negative Energy

☐ Poor Sleep Quality   ☐ Toxic Overload   ☐ Digital Device Overload

☐ Lack of Movement   ☐ Low Vibe Foods   ☐ Other/ Explain

High Vibe Checklist:

- [ ] Well Hydrated
- [ ] Great Sleep Quality
- [ ] Movement
- [ ] No Alcohol
- [ ] Low Toxic Input
- [ ] High Vibe Foods
- [ ] Positive Energy
- [ ] Digital Device Balance
- [ ] Other/Explain

I will use my creative magic by:

I will move my energy by:

Energy report:

Note from my higher self:

MY DAILY VIBE

Vibe I feel right now:

Vibe I want to feel:

5 things I am grateful for:

    1.

    2.

    3.

    4.

    5.

Draw your mood:

Low Vibe Checklist:

☐ Low Water Intake	☐ Alcohol	☐ Negative Energy
☐ Poor Sleep Quality	☐ Toxic Overload	☐ Digital Device Overload
☐ Lack of Movement	☐ Low Vibe Foods	☐ Other/ Explain

High Vibe Checklist:

☐ Well Hydrated ☐ No Alcohol ☐ Positive Energy

☐ Great Sleep Quality ☐ Low Toxic Input ☐ Digital Device Balance

☐ Movement ☐ High Vibe Foods ☐ Other/Explain

I will use my creative magic by:

I will move my energy by:

Energy report:

Note from my higher self:

MY DAILY VIBE

Vibe I feel right now:

Vibe I want to feel:

5 things I am grateful for:

1.

2.

3.

4.

5.

Draw your mood:

Low Vibe Checklist:

☐ Low Water Intake   ☐ Alcohol   ☐ Negative Energy

☐ Poor Sleep Quality   ☐ Toxic Overload   ☐ Digital Device Overload

☐ Lack of Movement   ☐ Low Vibe Foods   ☐ Other/ Explain

High Vibe Checklist:

- [ ] Well Hydrated
- [ ] Great Sleep Quality
- [ ] Movement
- [ ] No Alcohol
- [ ] Low Toxic Input
- [ ] High Vibe Foods
- [ ] Positive Energy
- [ ] Digital Device Balance
- [ ] Other/Explain

I will use my creative magic by:

I will move my energy by:

Energy report:

Note from my higher self:

MY DAILY VIBE

Vibe I feel right now:

Vibe I want to feel:

5 things I am grateful for:

1.

2.

3.

4.

5.

Draw your mood:

Low Vibe Checklist:

☐ Low Water Intake   ☐ Alcohol   ☐ Negative Energy

☐ Poor Sleep Quality   ☐ Toxic Overload   ☐ Digital Device Overload

☐ Lack of Movement   ☐ Low Vibe Foods   ☐ Other/ Explain

High Vibe Checklist:

- [ ] Well Hydrated
- [ ] Great Sleep Quality
- [ ] Movement
- [ ] No Alcohol
- [ ] Low Toxic Input
- [ ] High Vibe Foods
- [ ] Positive Energy
- [ ] Digital Device Balance
- [ ] Other/Explain

I will use my creative magic by:

I will move my energy by:

Energy report:

Note from my higher self:

MY DAILY VIBE

Vibe I feel right now:

Vibe I want to feel:

5 things I am grateful for:

1.

2.

3.

4.

5.

Draw your mood:

Low Vibe Checklist:

☐ Low Water Intake	☐ Alcohol	☐ Negative Energy
☐ Poor Sleep Quality	☐ Toxic Overload	☐ Digital Device Overload
☐ Lack of Movement	☐ Low Vibe Foods	☐ Other/ Explain

High Vibe Checklist:

- ☐ Well Hydrated
- ☐ No Alcohol
- ☐ Positive Energy
- ☐ Great Sleep Quality
- ☐ Low Toxic Input
- ☐ Digital Device Balance
- ☐ Movement
- ☐ High Vibe Foods
- ☐ Other/Explain

I will use my creative magic by:

I will move my energy by:

Energy report:

Note from my higher self:

MY DAILY VIBE

Vibe I feel right now:

Vibe I want to feel:

5 things I am grateful for:

1.

2.

3.

4.

5.

Draw your mood:

Low Vibe Checklist:

☐ Low Water Intake

☐ Alcohol

☐ Negative Energy

☐ Poor Sleep Quality

☐ Toxic Overload

☐ Digital Device Overload

☐ Lack of Movement

☐ Low Vibe Foods

☐ Other/ Explain

High Vibe Checklist:

- ☐ Well Hydrated
- ☐ Great Sleep Quality
- ☐ Movement
- ☐ No Alcohol
- ☐ Low Toxic Input
- ☐ High Vibe Foods
- ☐ Positive Energy
- ☐ Digital Device Balance
- ☐ Other/Explain

I will use my creative magic by:

I will move my energy by:

Energy report:

Note from my higher self:

MY DAILY VIBE

Vibe I feel right now:

Vibe I want to feel:

5 things I am grateful for:

1.

2.

3.

4.

5.

Draw your mood:

Low Vibe Checklist:

☐ Low Water Intake ☐ Alcohol ☐ Negative Energy

☐ Poor Sleep Quality ☐ Toxic Overload ☐ Digital Device Overload

☐ Lack of Movement ☐ Low Vibe Foods ☐ Other/ Explain

High Vibe Checklist:

☐ Well Hydrated ☐ No Alcohol ☐ Positive Energy

☐ Great Sleep Quality ☐ Low Toxic Input ☐ Digital Device Balance

☐ Movement ☐ High Vibe Foods ☐ Other/Explain

I will use my creative magic by:

I will move my energy by:

Energy report:

Note from my higher self:

MY
DAILY
VIBE

Vibe I feel right now:

Vibe I want to feel:

5 things I am grateful for:

    1.

    2.

    3.

    4.

    5.

Draw your mood:

Low Vibe Checklist:

☐	Low Water Intake	☐	Alcohol	☐	Negative Energy
☐	Poor Sleep Quality	☐	Toxic Overload	☐	Digital Device Overload
☐	Lack of Movement	☐	Low Vibe Foods	☐	Other/ Explain

High Vibe Checklist:

- [ ] Well Hydrated
- [ ] No Alcohol
- [ ] Positive Energy
- [ ] Great Sleep Quality
- [ ] Low Toxic Input
- [ ] Digital Device Balance
- [ ] Movement
- [ ] High Vibe Foods
- [ ] Other/Explain

I will use my creative magic by:

I will move my energy by:

Energy report:

Note from my higher self:

MY DAILY VIBE

Vibe I feel right now:

Vibe I want to feel:

5 things I am grateful for:

    1.

    2.

    3.

    4.

    5.

Draw your mood:

Low Vibe Checklist:

☐ Low Water Intake   ☐ Alcohol   ☐ Negative Energy

☐ Poor Sleep Quality   ☐ Toxic Overload   ☐ Digital Device Overload

☐ Lack of Movement   ☐ Low Vibe Foods   ☐ Other/ Explain

High Vibe Checklist:

☐ Well Hydrated ☐ No Alcohol ☐ Positive Energy

☐ Great Sleep Quality ☐ Low Toxic Input ☐ Digital Device Balance

☐ Movement ☐ High Vibe Foods ☐ Other/Explain

I will use my creative magic by:

I will move my energy by:

Energy report:

Note from my higher self:

MY
DAILY
VIBE

Vibe I feel right now:

Vibe I want to feel:

5 things I am grateful for:

    1.

    2.

    3.

    4.

    5.

Draw your mood:

Low Vibe Checklist:

☐ Low Water Intake	☐ Alcohol	☐ Negative Energy
☐ Poor Sleep Quality	☐ Toxic Overload	☐ Digital Device Overload
☐ Lack of Movement	☐ Low Vibe Foods	☐ Other/ Explain

High Vibe Checklist:

☐ Well Hydrated   ☐ No Alcohol   ☐ Positive Energy

☐ Great Sleep Quality   ☐ Low Toxic Input   ☐ Digital Device Balance

☐ Movement   ☐ High Vibe Foods   ☐ Other/Explain

I will use my creative magic by:

I will move my energy by:

Energy report:

Note from my higher self:

MY
DAILY
VIBE

Vibe I feel right now:

Vibe I want to feel:

5 things I am grateful for:

    1.

    2.

    3.

    4.

    5.

Draw your mood:

Low Vibe Checklist:

☐ Low Water Intake	☐ Alcohol	☐ Negative Energy
☐ Poor Sleep Quality	☐ Toxic Overload	☐ Digital Device Overload
☐ Lack of Movement	☐ Low Vibe Foods	☐ Other/ Explain

High Vibe Checklist:

☐ Well Hydrated ☐ No Alcohol ☐ Positive Energy

☐ Great Sleep Quality ☐ Low Toxic Input ☐ Digital Device Balance

☐ Movement ☐ High Vibe Foods ☐ Other/Explain

I will use my creative magic by:

I will move my energy by:

Energy report:

Note from my higher self:

MY DAILY VIBE

Vibe I feel right now:

Vibe I want to feel:

5 things I am grateful for:

    1.

    2.

    3.

    4.

    5.

Draw your mood:

Low Vibe Checklist:

☐	Low Water Intake	☐	Alcohol	☐	Negative Energy
☐	Poor Sleep Quality	☐	Toxic Overload	☐	Digital Device Overload
☐	Lack of Movement	☐	Low Vibe Foods	☐	Other/ Explain

High Vibe Checklist:

- [ ] Well Hydrated
- [ ] No Alcohol
- [ ] Positive Energy
- [ ] Great Sleep Quality
- [ ] Low Toxic Input
- [ ] Digital Device Balance
- [ ] Movement
- [ ] High Vibe Foods
- [ ] Other/Explain

I will use my creative magic by:

I will move my energy by:

Energy report:

Note from my higher self:

MY DAILY VIBE

Vibe I feel right now:

Vibe I want to feel:

5 things I am grateful for:

1.

2.

3.

4.

5.

Draw your mood:

Low Vibe Checklist:

☐ Low Water Intake   ☐ Alcohol   ☐ Negative Energy

☐ Poor Sleep Quality   ☐ Toxic Overload   ☐ Digital Device Overload

☐ Lack of Movement   ☐ Low Vibe Foods   ☐ Other/ Explain

High Vibe Checklist:

☐ Well Hydrated   ☐ No Alcohol   ☐ Positive Energy

☐ Great Sleep Quality   ☐ Low Toxic Input   ☐ Digital Device Balance

☐ Movement   ☐ High Vibe Foods   ☐ Other/Explain

I will use my creative magic by:

I will move my energy by:

Energy report:

Note from my higher self:

MY
DAILY
VIBE

Vibe I feel right now:

Vibe I want to feel:

5 things I am grateful for:

1.

2.

3.

4.

5.

Draw your mood:

Low Vibe Checklist:

☐ Low Water Intake   ☐ Alcohol   ☐ Negative Energy

☐ Poor Sleep Quality   ☐ Toxic Overload   ☐ Digital Device Overload

☐ Lack of Movement   ☐ Low Vibe Foods   ☐ Other/ Explain

High Vibe Checklist:

☐ Well Hydrated   ☐ No Alcohol   ☐ Positive Energy

☐ Great Sleep Quality   ☐ Low Toxic Input   ☐ Digital Device Balance

☐ Movement   ☐ High Vibe Foods   ☐ Other/Explain

I will use my creative magic by:

I will move my energy by:

Energy report:

Note from my higher self:

MY DAILY VIBE

Vibe I feel right now:

Vibe I want to feel:

5 things I am grateful for:

1.

2.

3.

4.

5.

Draw your mood:

Low Vibe Checklist:

☐ Low Water Intake ☐ Alcohol ☐ Negative Energy

☐ Poor Sleep Quality ☐ Toxic Overload ☐ Digital Device Overload

☐ Lack of Movement ☐ Low Vibe Foods ☐ Other/ Explain

High Vibe Checklist:

- ☐ Well Hydrated
- ☐ Great Sleep Quality
- ☐ Movement

- ☐ No Alcohol
- ☐ Low Toxic Input
- ☐ High Vibe Foods

- ☐ Positive Energy
- ☐ Digital Device Balance
- ☐ Other/Explain

I will use my creative magic by:

I will move my energy by:

Energy report:

Note from my higher self:

MY
DAILY
VIBE

Vibe I feel right now:

Vibe I want to feel:

5 things I am grateful for:

1.

2.

3.

4.

5.

Draw your mood:

Low Vibe Checklist:

☐ Low Water Intake ☐ Alcohol ☐ Negative Energy

☐ Poor Sleep Quality ☐ Toxic Overload ☐ Digital Device Overload

☐ Lack of Movement ☐ Low Vibe Foods ☐ Other/ Explain

High Vibe Checklist:

- [ ] Well Hydrated
- [ ] No Alcohol
- [ ] Positive Energy
- [ ] Great Sleep Quality
- [ ] Low Toxic Input
- [ ] Digital Device Balance
- [ ] Movement
- [ ] High Vibe Foods
- [ ] Other/Explain

I will use my creative magic by:

I will move my energy by:

Energy report:

Note from my higher self:

MY DAILY VIBE

Vibe I feel right now:

Vibe I want to feel:

5 things I am grateful for:

1.

2.

3.

4.

5.

Draw your mood:

Low Vibe Checklist:

☐ Low Water Intake

☐ Poor Sleep Quality

☐ Lack of Movement

☐ Alcohol

☐ Toxic Overload

☐ Low Vibe Foods

☐ Negative Energy

☐ Digital Device Overload

☐ Other/ Explain

High Vibe Checklist:

- ☐ Well Hydrated
- ☐ Great Sleep Quality
- ☐ Movement

- ☐ No Alcohol
- ☐ Low Toxic Input
- ☐ High Vibe Foods

- ☐ Positive Energy
- ☐ Digital Device Balance
- ☐ Other/Explain

I will use my creative magic by:

I will move my energy by:

Energy report:

Note from my higher self:

MY DAILY VIBE

Vibe I feel right now:

Vibe I want to feel:

5 things I am grateful for:

1.

2.

3.

4.

5.

Draw your mood:

Low Vibe Checklist:

☐ Low Water Intake   ☐ Alcohol   ☐ Negative Energy

☐ Poor Sleep Quality   ☐ Toxic Overload   ☐ Digital Device Overload

☐ Lack of Movement   ☐ Low Vibe Foods   ☐ Other/ Explain

High Vibe Checklist:

☐ Well Hydrated ☐ No Alcohol ☐ Positive Energy

☐ Great Sleep Quality ☐ Low Toxic Input ☐ Digital Device Balance

☐ Movement ☐ High Vibe Foods ☐ Other/Explain

I will use my creative magic by:

I will move my energy by:

Energy report:

Note from my higher self:

MY
DAILY
VIBE

Vibe I feel right now:

Vibe I want to feel:

5 things I am grateful for:

    1.

    2.

    3.

    4.

    5.

Draw your mood:

Low Vibe Checklist:

☐ Low Water Intake

☐ Alcohol

☐ Negative Energy

☐ Poor Sleep Quality

☐ Toxic Overload

☐ Digital Device Overload

☐ Lack of Movement

☐ Low Vibe Foods

☐ Other/ Explain

High Vibe Checklist:

☐ Well Hydrated   ☐ No Alcohol   ☐ Positive Energy

☐ Great Sleep Quality   ☐ Low Toxic Input   ☐ Digital Device Balance

☐ Movement   ☐ High Vibe Foods   ☐ Other/Explain

I will use my creative magic by:

I will move my energy by:

Energy report:

Note from my higher self:

MY DAILY VIBE

Vibe I feel right now:

Vibe I want to feel:

5 things I am grateful for:

    1.

    2.

    3.

    4.

    5.

Draw your mood:

Low Vibe Checklist:

☐	Low Water Intake	☐	Alcohol	☐	Negative Energy
☐	Poor Sleep Quality	☐	Toxic Overload	☐	Digital Device Overload
☐	Lack of Movement	☐	Low Vibe Foods	☐	Other/ Explain

High Vibe Checklist:

- [ ] Well Hydrated
- [ ] Great Sleep Quality
- [ ] Movement
- [ ] No Alcohol
- [ ] Low Toxic Input
- [ ] High Vibe Foods
- [ ] Positive Energy
- [ ] Digital Device Balance
- [ ] Other/Explain

I will use my creative magic by:

I will move my energy by:

Energy report:

Note from my higher self:

MY DAILY VIBE

Vibe I feel right now:

Vibe I want to feel:

5 things I am grateful for:

    1.

    2.

    3.

    4.

    5.

Draw your mood:

Low Vibe Checklist:

☐ Low Water Intake	☐ Alcohol	☐ Negative Energy
☐ Poor Sleep Quality	☐ Toxic Overload	☐ Digital Device Overload
☐ Lack of Movement	☐ Low Vibe Foods	☐ Other/ Explain

High Vibe Checklist:

☐ Well Hydrated   ☐ No Alcohol   ☐ Positive Energy

☐ Great Sleep Quality   ☐ Low Toxic Input   ☐ Digital Device Balance

☐ Movement   ☐ High Vibe Foods   ☐ Other/Explain

I will use my creative magic by:

I will move my energy by:

Energy report:

Note from my higher self:

MY
DAILY
VIBE

Vibe I feel right now:

Vibe I want to feel:

5 things I am grateful for:

1.

2.

3.

4.

5.

Draw your mood:

Low Vibe Checklist:

☐ Low Water Intake   ☐ Alcohol   ☐ Negative Energy

☐ Poor Sleep Quality   ☐ Toxic Overload   ☐ Digital Device Overload

☐ Lack of Movement   ☐ Low Vibe Foods   ☐ Other/ Explain

High Vibe Checklist:

- ☐ Well Hydrated
- ☐ Great Sleep Quality
- ☐ Movement
- ☐ No Alcohol
- ☐ Low Toxic Input
- ☐ High Vibe Foods
- ☐ Positive Energy
- ☐ Digital Device Balance
- ☐ Other/Explain

I will use my creative magic by:

I will move my energy by:

Energy report:

Note from my higher self:

MY DAILY VIBE

Vibe I feel right now:

Vibe I want to feel:

5 things I am grateful for:

    1.

    2.

    3.

    4.

    5.

Draw your mood:

Low Vibe Checklist:

☐ Low Water Intake	☐ Alcohol	☐ Negative Energy
☐ Poor Sleep Quality	☐ Toxic Overload	☐ Digital Device Overload
☐ Lack of Movement	☐ Low Vibe Foods	☐ Other/ Explain

High Vibe Checklist:

- ☐ Well Hydrated
- ☐ Great Sleep Quality
- ☐ Movement
- ☐ No Alcohol
- ☐ Low Toxic Input
- ☐ High Vibe Foods
- ☐ Positive Energy
- ☐ Digital Device Balance
- ☐ Other/Explain

I will use my creative magic by:

I will move my energy by:

Energy report:

Note from my higher self:

MY DAILY VIBE

Vibe I feel right now:

Vibe I want to feel:

5 things I am grateful for:

1.

2.

3.

4.

5.

Draw your mood:

Low Vibe Checklist:

☐ Low Water Intake   ☐ Alcohol   ☐ Negative Energy

☐ Poor Sleep Quality   ☐ Toxic Overload   ☐ Digital Device Overload

☐ Lack of Movement   ☐ Low Vibe Foods   ☐ Other/ Explain

High Vibe Checklist:

- ☐ Well Hydrated
- ☐ Great Sleep Quality
- ☐ Movement

- ☐ No Alcohol
- ☐ Low Toxic Input
- ☐ High Vibe Foods

- ☐ Positive Energy
- ☐ Digital Device Balance
- ☐ Other/Explain

I will use my creative magic by:

I will move my energy by:

Energy report:

Note from my higher self:

MY DAILY VIBE

Vibe I feel right now:

Vibe I want to feel:

5 things I am grateful for:

1.

2.

3.

4.

5.

Draw your mood:

Low Vibe Checklist:

☐ Low Water Intake	☐ Alcohol	☐ Negative Energy
☐ Poor Sleep Quality	☐ Toxic Overload	☐ Digital Device Overload
☐ Lack of Movement	☐ Low Vibe Foods	☐ Other/ Explain

High Vibe Checklist:

- [ ] Well Hydrated
- [ ] Great Sleep Quality
- [ ] Movement

- [ ] No Alcohol
- [ ] Low Toxic Input
- [ ] High Vibe Foods

- [ ] Positive Energy
- [ ] Digital Device Balance
- [ ] Other/Explain

I will use my creative magic by:

I will move my energy by:

Energy report:

Note from my higher self:

MY
DAILY
VIBE

Vibe I feel right now:

Vibe I want to feel:

5 things I am grateful for:

    1.

    2.

    3.

    4.

    5.

Draw your mood:

Low Vibe Checklist:

- ☐ Low Water Intake
- ☐ Alcohol
- ☐ Negative Energy
- ☐ Poor Sleep Quality
- ☐ Toxic Overload
- ☐ Digital Device Overload
- ☐ Lack of Movement
- ☐ Low Vibe Foods
- ☐ Other/ Explain

High Vibe Checklist:

- [ ] Well Hydrated
- [ ] Great Sleep Quality
- [ ] Movement
- [ ] No Alcohol
- [ ] Low Toxic Input
- [ ] High Vibe Foods
- [ ] Positive Energy
- [ ] Digital Device Balance
- [ ] Other/Explain

I will use my creative magic by:

I will move my energy by:

Energy report:

Note from my higher self:

MY DAILY VIBE

Vibe I feel right now:

Vibe I want to feel:

5 things I am grateful for:

    1.

    2.

    3.

    4.

    5.

Draw your mood:

Low Vibe Checklist:

☐ Low Water Intake   ☐ Alcohol   ☐ Negative Energy

☐ Poor Sleep Quality   ☐ Toxic Overload   ☐ Digital Device Overload

☐ Lack of Movement   ☐ Low Vibe Foods   ☐ Other/ Explain

High Vibe Checklist:

☐ Well Hydrated   ☐ No Alcohol   ☐ Positive Energy

☐ Great Sleep Quality   ☐ Low Toxic Input   ☐ Digital Device Balance

☐ Movement   ☐ High Vibe Foods   ☐ Other/Explain

I will use my creative magic by:

I will move my energy by:

Energy report:

Note from my higher self:

MY
DAILY
VIBE

Vibe I feel right now:

Vibe I want to feel:

5 things I am grateful for:

    1.

    2.

    3.

    4.

    5.

Draw your mood:

Low Vibe Checklist:

☐ Low Water Intake	☐ Alcohol	☐ Negative Energy
☐ Poor Sleep Quality	☐ Toxic Overload	☐ Digital Device Overload
☐ Lack of Movement	☐ Low Vibe Foods	☐ Other/ Explain

High Vibe Checklist:

☐ Well Hydrated ☐ No Alcohol ☐ Positive Energy

☐ Great Sleep Quality ☐ Low Toxic Input ☐ Digital Device Balance

☐ Movement ☐ High Vibe Foods ☐ Other/Explain

I will use my creative magic by:

I will move my energy by:

Energy report:

Note from my higher self:

MY
DAILY
VIBE

Vibe I feel right now:

Vibe I want to feel:

5 things I am grateful for:

    1.

    2.

    3.

    4.

    5.

Draw your mood:

Low Vibe Checklist:

☐ Low Water Intake   ☐ Alcohol   ☐ Negative Energy

☐ Poor Sleep Quality   ☐ Toxic Overload   ☐ Digital Device Overload

☐ Lack of Movement   ☐ Low Vibe Foods   ☐ Other/ Explain

High Vibe Checklist:

☐ Well Hydrated ☐ No Alcohol ☐ Positive Energy

☐ Great Sleep Quality ☐ Low Toxic Input ☐ Digital Device Balance

☐ Movement ☐ High Vibe Foods ☐ Other/Explain

I will use my creative magic by:

I will move my energy by:

Energy report:

Note from my higher self:

MY DAILY VIBE

Vibe I feel right now:

Vibe I want to feel:

5 things I am grateful for:

1.

2.

3.

4.

5.

Draw your mood:

Low Vibe Checklist:

☐ Low Water Intake   ☐ Alcohol   ☐ Negative Energy

☐ Poor Sleep Quality   ☐ Toxic Overload   ☐ Digital Device Overload

☐ Lack of Movement   ☐ Low Vibe Foods   ☐ Other/ Explain

High Vibe Checklist:

☐ Well Hydrated ☐ No Alcohol ☐ Positive Energy

☐ Great Sleep Quality ☐ Low Toxic Input ☐ Digital Device Balance

☐ Movement ☐ High Vibe Foods ☐ Other/Explain

I will use my creative magic by:

I will move my energy by:

Energy report:

Note from my higher self:

MY DAILY VIBE

Vibe I feel right now:

Vibe I want to feel:

5 things I am grateful for:

1.

2.

3.

4.

5.

Draw your mood:

Low Vibe Checklist:

☐ Low Water Intake   ☐ Alcohol   ☐ Negative Energy

☐ Poor Sleep Quality   ☐ Toxic Overload   ☐ Digital Device Overload

☐ Lack of Movement   ☐ Low Vibe Foods   ☐ Other/ Explain

High Vibe Checklist:

- [ ] Well Hydrated
- [ ] No Alcohol
- [ ] Positive Energy
- [ ] Great Sleep Quality
- [ ] Low Toxic Input
- [ ] Digital Device Balance
- [ ] Movement
- [ ] High Vibe Foods
- [ ] Other/Explain

I will use my creative magic by:

I will move my energy by:

Energy report:

Note from my higher self:

MY
DAILY
VIBE

Vibe I feel right now:

Vibe I want to feel:

5 things I am grateful for:

1.

2.

3.

4.

5.

Draw your mood:

Low Vibe Checklist:

☐ Low Water
Intake

☐ Alcohol

☐ Negative
Energy

☐ Poor Sleep
Quality

☐ Toxic
Overload

☐ Digital Device
Overload

☐ Lack of
Movement

☐ Low Vibe
Foods

☐ Other/
Explain

High Vibe Checklist:

☐ Well Hydrated   ☐ No Alcohol   ☐ Positive Energy

☐ Great Sleep Quality   ☐ Low Toxic Input   ☐ Digital Device Balance

☐ Movement   ☐ High Vibe Foods   ☐ Other/Explain

I will use my creative magic by:

I will move my energy by:

Energy report:

Note from my higher self:

MY
DAILY
VIBE

Vibe I feel right now:

Vibe I want to feel:

5 things I am grateful for:

    1.

    2.

    3.

    4.

    5.

Draw your mood:

Low Vibe Checklist:

☐ Low Water Intake	☐ Alcohol	☐ Negative Energy
☐ Poor Sleep Quality	☐ Toxic Overload	☐ Digital Device Overload
☐ Lack of Movement	☐ Low Vibe Foods	☐ Other/ Explain

High Vibe Checklist:

☐ Well Hydrated ☐ No Alcohol ☐ Positive Energy

☐ Great Sleep Quality ☐ Low Toxic Innput ☐ Digital Device Balance

☐ Movement ☐ High Vibe Foods ☐ Other/Explain

I will use my creative magic by:

I will move my energy by:

Energy report:

Note from my higher self:

MY DAILY VIBE

Vibe I feel right now:

Vibe I want to feel:

5 things I am grateful for:

    1.

    2.

    3.

    4.

    5.

Draw your mood:

Low Vibe Checklist:

- [ ] Low Water Intake
- [ ] Poor Sleep Quality
- [ ] Lack of Movement
- [ ] Alcohol
- [ ] Toxic Overload
- [ ] Low Vibe Foods
- [ ] Negative Energy
- [ ] Digital Device Overload
- [ ] Other/ Explain

High Vibe Checklist:

- [ ] Well Hydrated
- [ ] Great Sleep Quality
- [ ] Movement
- [ ] No Alcohol
- [ ] Low Toxic Input
- [ ] High Vibe Foods
- [ ] Positive Energy
- [ ] Digital Device Balance
- [ ] Other/Explain

I will use my creative magic by:

I will move my energy by:

Energy report:

Note from my higher self:

MY DAILY VIBE

Vibe I feel right now:

Vibe I want to feel:

5 things I am grateful for:

    1.

    2.

    3.

    4.

    5.

Draw your mood:

Low Vibe Checklist:

☐ Low Water Intake	☐ Alcohol	☐ Negative Energy
☐ Poor Sleep Quality	☐ Toxic Overload	☐ Digital Device Overload
☐ Lack of Movement	☐ Low Vibe Foods	☐ Other/ Explain

High Vibe Checklist:

☐ Well Hydrated ☐ No Alcohol ☐ Positive Energy

☐ Great Sleep Quality ☐ Low Toxic Input ☐ Digital Device Balance

☐ Movement ☐ High Vibe Foods ☐ Other/Explain

I will use my creative magic by:

I will move my energy by:

Energy report:

Note from my higher self:

MY DAILY VIBE

Vibe I feel right now:

Vibe I want to feel:

5 things I am grateful for:

1.

2.

3.

4.

5.

Draw your mood:

Low Vibe Checklist:

☐ Low Water Intake   ☐ Alcohol   ☐ Negative Energy

☐ Poor Sleep Quality   ☐ Toxic Overload   ☐ Digital Device Overload

☐ Lack of Movement   ☐ Low Vibe Foods   ☐ Other/ Explain

High Vibe Checklist:

☐ Well Hydrated	☐ No Alcohol	☐ Positive Energy
☐ Great Sleep Quality	☐ Low Toxic Input	☐ Digital Device Balance
☐ Movement	☐ High Vibe Foods	☐ Other/Explain

I will use my creative magic by:

I will move my energy by:

Energy report:

Note from my higher self:

MY DAILY VIBE

Vibe I feel right now:

Vibe I want to feel:

5 things I am grateful for:

1.

2.

3.

4.

5.

Draw your mood:

Low Vibe Checklist:

☐ Low Water Intake   ☐ Alcohol   ☐ Negative Energy

☐ Poor Sleep Quality   ☐ Toxic Overload   ☐ Digital Device Overload

☐ Lack of Movement   ☐ Low Vibe Foods   ☐ Other/ Explain

High Vibe Checklist:

☐ Well Hydrated   ☐ No Alcohol   ☐ Positive Energy

☐ Great Sleep Quality   ☐ Low Toxic Input   ☐ Digital Device Balance

☐ Movement   ☐ High Vibe Foods   ☐ Other/Explain

I will use my creative magic by:

I will move my energy by:

Energy report:

Note from my higher self:

MY DAILY VIBE

Vibe I feel right now:

Vibe I want to feel:

5 things I am grateful for:

    1.

    2.

    3.

    4.

    5.

Draw your mood:

Low Vibe Checklist:

☐ Low Water Intake	☐ Alcohol	☐ Negative Energy
☐ Poor Sleep Quality	☐ Toxic Overload	☐ Digital Device Overload
☐ Lack of Movement	☐ Low Vibe Foods	☐ Other/ Explain

High Vibe Checklist:

☐ Well Hydrated ☐ No Alcohol ☐ Positive Energy

☐ Great Sleep Quality ☐ Low Toxic Input ☐ Digital Device Balance

☐ Movement ☐ High Vibe Foods ☐ Other/Explain

I will use my creative magic by:

I will move my energy by:

Energy report:

Note from my higher self:

MY DAILY VIBE

Vibe I feel right now:

Vibe I want to feel:

5 things I am grateful for:

    1.

    2.

    3.

    4.

    5.

Draw your mood:

Low Vibe Checklist:

☐ Low Water Intake	☐ Alcohol	☐ Negative Energy
☐ Poor Sleep Quality	☐ Toxic Overload	☐ Digital Device Overload
☐ Lack of Movement	☐ Low Vibe Foods	☐ Other/ Explain

High Vibe Checklist:

- [ ] Well Hydrated
- [ ] Great Sleep Quality
- [ ] Movement
- [ ] No Alcohol
- [ ] Low Toxic Input
- [ ] High Vibe Foods
- [ ] Positive Energy
- [ ] Digital Device Balance
- [ ] Other/Explain

I will use my creative magic by:

I will move my energy by:

Energy report:

Note from my higher self:

MY DAILY VIBE

Vibe I feel right now:

Vibe I want to feel:

5 things I am grateful for:

    1.

    2.

    3.

    4.

    5.

Draw your mood:

Low Vibe Checklist:

☐ Low Water Intake	☐ Alcohol	☐ Negative Energy
☐ Poor Sleep Quality	☐ Toxic Overload	☐ Digital Device Overload
☐ Lack of Movement	☐ Low Vibe Foods	☐ Other/ Explain

High Vibe Checklist:

- ☐ Well Hydrated
- ☐ No Alcohol
- ☐ Positive Energy
- ☐ Great Sleep Quality
- ☐ Low Toxic Input
- ☐ Digital Device Balance
- ☐ Movement
- ☐ High Vibe Foods
- ☐ Other/Explain

I will use my creative magic by:

I will move my energy by:

Energy report:

Note from my higher self:

MY DAILY VIBE

Vibe I feel right now:

Vibe I want to feel:

5 things I am grateful for:

    1.

    2.

    3.

    4.

    5.

Draw your mood:

Low Vibe Checklist:

- ☐ Low Water Intake
- ☐ Alcohol
- ☐ Negative Energy
- ☐ Poor Sleep Quality
- ☐ Toxic Overload
- ☐ Digital Device Overload
- ☐ Lack of Movement
- ☐ Low Vibe Foods
- ☐ Other/ Explain

High Vibe Checklist:

- [ ] Well Hydrated
- [ ] Great Sleep Quality
- [ ] Movement
- [ ] No Alcohol
- [ ] Low Toxic Input
- [ ] High Vibe Foods
- [ ] Positive Energy
- [ ] Digital Device Balance
- [ ] Other/Explain

I will use my creative magic by:

I will move my energy by:

Energy report:

Note from my higher self:

MY DAILY VIBE

Vibe I feel right now:

Vibe I want to feel:

5 things I am grateful for:

1.

2.

3.

4.

5.

Draw your mood:

Low Vibe Checklist:

☐ Low Water Intake

☐ Alcohol

☐ Negative Energy

☐ Poor Sleep Quality

☐ Toxic Overload

☐ Digital Device Overload

☐ Lack of Movement

☐ Low Vibe Foods

☐ Other/ Explain

High Vibe Checklist:

☐ Well Hydrated　　☐ No Alcohol　　☐ Positive Energy

☐ Great Sleep Quality　　☐ Low Toxic Input　　☐ Digital Device Balance

☐ Movement　　☐ High Vibe Foods　　☐ Other/Explain

I will use my creative magic by:

I will move my energy by:

Energy report:

Note from my higher self:

MY DAILY VIBE

Vibe I feel right now:

Vibe I want to feel:

5 things I am grateful for:

1.

2.

3.

4.

5.

Draw your mood:

Low Vibe Checklist:

☐ Low Water Intake   ☐ Alcohol   ☐ Negative Energy

☐ Poor Sleep Quality   ☐ Toxic Overload   ☐ Digital Device Overload

☐ Lack of Movement   ☐ Low Vibe Foods   ☐ Other/ Explain

High Vibe Checklist:

- ☐ Well Hydrated
- ☐ No Alcohol
- ☐ Positive Energy
- ☐ Great Sleep Quality
- ☐ Low Toxic Input
- ☐ Digital Device Balance
- ☐ Movement
- ☐ High Vibe Foods
- ☐ Other/Explain

I will use my creative magic by:

I will move my energy by:

Energy report:

Note from my higher self:

MY DAILY VIBE

Vibe I feel right now:

Vibe I want to feel:

5 things I am grateful for:

1.

2.

3.

4.

5.

Draw your mood:

Low Vibe Checklist:

☐ Low Water Intake   ☐ Alcohol   ☐ Negative Energy

☐ Poor Sleep Quality   ☐ Toxic Overload   ☐ Digital Device Overload

☐ Lack of Movement   ☐ Low Vibe Foods   ☐ Other/ Explain

High Vibe Checklist:

☐ Well Hydrated ☐ No Alcohol ☐ Positive Energy

☐ Great Sleep Quality ☐ Low Toxic Input ☐ Digital Device Balance

☐ Movement ☐ High Vibe Foods ☐ Other/Explain

I will use my creative magic by:

I will move my energy by:

Energy report:

Note from my higher self:

MY DAILY VIBE

Vibe I feel right now:

Vibe I want to feel:

5 things I am grateful for:

    1.

    2.

    3.

    4.

    5.

Draw your mood:

Low Vibe Checklist:

☐ Low Water Intake	☐ Alcohol	☐ Negative Energy
☐ Poor Sleep Quality	☐ Toxic Overload	☐ Digital Device Overload
☐ Lack of Movement	☐ Low Vibe Foods	☐ Other/ Explain

High Vibe Checklist:

- [ ] Well Hydrated
- [ ] Great Sleep Quality
- [ ] Movement
- [ ] No Alcohol
- [ ] Low Toxic Input
- [ ] High Vibe Foods
- [ ] Positive Energy
- [ ] Digital Device Balance
- [ ] Other/Explain

I will use my creative magic by:

I will move my energy by:

Energy report:

Note from my higher self:

MY
DAILY
VIBE

Vibe I feel right now:

Vibe I want to feel:

5 things I am grateful for:

    1.

    2.

    3.

    4.

    5.

Draw your mood:

Low Vibe Checklist:

☐ Low Water Intake   ☐ Alcohol   ☐ Negative Energy

☐ Poor Sleep Quality   ☐ Toxic Overload   ☐ Digital Device Overload

☐ Lack of Movement   ☐ Low Vibe Foods   ☐ Other/ Explain

High Vibe Checklist:

- ☐ Well Hydrated
- ☐ No Alcohol
- ☐ Positive Energy
- ☐ Great Sleep Quality
- ☐ Low Toxic Input
- ☐ Digital Device Balance
- ☐ Movement
- ☐ High Vibe Foods
- ☐ Other/Explain

I will use my creative magic by:

I will move my energy by:

Energy report:

Note from my higher self:

MY DAILY VIBE

Vibe I feel right now:

Vibe I want to feel:

5 things I am grateful for:

    1.

    2.

    3.

    4.

    5.

Draw your mood:

Low Vibe Checklist:

☐ Low Water Intake	☐ Alcohol	☐ Negative Energy
☐ Poor Sleep Quality	☐ Toxic Overload	☐ Digital Device Overload
☐ Lack of Movement	☐ Low Vibe Foods	☐ Other/ Explain

High Vibe Checklist:

☐ Well Hydrated ☐ No Alcohol ☐ Positive Energy

☐ Great Sleep Quality ☐ Low Toxic Input ☐ Digital Device Balance

☐ Movement ☐ High Vibe Foods ☐ Other/Explain

I will use my creative magic by:

I will move my energy by:

Energy report:

Note from my higher self:

MY
DAILY
VIBE

Vibe I feel right now:

Vibe I want to feel:

5 things I am grateful for:

    1.

    2.

    3.

    4.

    5.

Draw your mood:

Low Vibe Checklist:

☐ Low Water Intake	☐ Alcohol	☐ Negative Energy
☐ Poor Sleep Quality	☐ Toxic Overload	☐ Digital Device Overload
☐ Lack of Movement	☐ Low Vibe Foods	☐ Other/ Explain

High Vibe Checklist:

☐ Well Hydrated   ☐ No Alcohol   ☐ Positive Energy

☐ Great Sleep Quality   ☐ Low Toxic Input   ☐ Digital Device Balance

☐ Movement   ☐ High Vibe Foods   ☐ Other/Explain

I will use my creative magic by:

I will move my energy by:

Energy report:

Note from my higher self:

MY DAILY VIBE

Vibe I feel right now:

Vibe I want to feel:

5 things I am grateful for:

    1.

    2.

    3.

    4.

    5.

Draw your mood:

Low Vibe Checklist:

- ☐ Low Water Intake
- ☐ Poor Sleep Quality
- ☐ Lack of Movement
- ☐ Alcohol
- ☐ Toxic Overload
- ☐ Low Vibe Foods
- ☐ Negative Energy
- ☐ Digital Device Overload
- ☐ Other/ Explain

High Vibe Checklist:

- ☐ Well Hydrated
- ☐ No Alcohol
- ☐ Positive Energy
- ☐ Great Sleep Quality
- ☐ Low Toxic Input
- ☐ Digital Device Balance
- ☐ Movement
- ☐ High Vibe Foods
- ☐ Other/Explain

I will use my creative magic by:

I will move my energy by:

Energy report:

Note from my higher self:

MY DAILY VIBE

Vibe I feel right now:

Vibe I want to feel:

5 things I am grateful for:

1.

2.

3.

4.

5.

Draw your mood:

Low Vibe Checklist:

☐ Low Water Intake   ☐ Alcohol   ☐ Negative Energy

☐ Poor Sleep Quality   ☐ Toxic Overload   ☐ Digital Device Overload

☐ Lack of Movement   ☐ Low Vibe Foods   ☐ Other/ Explain

High Vibe Checklist:

☐ Well Hydrated   ☐ No Alcohol   ☐ Positive Energy

☐ Great Sleep Quality   ☐ Low Toxic Input   ☐ Digital Device Balance

☐ Movement   ☐ High Vibe Foods   ☐ Other/Explain

I will use my creative magic by:

I will move my energy by:

Energy report:

Note from my higher self:

MY DAILY VIBE

Vibe I feel right now:

Vibe I want to feel:

5 things I am grateful for:

    1.

    2.

    3.

    4.

    5.

Draw your mood:

Low Vibe Checklist:

☐ Low Water Intake   ☐ Alcohol   ☐ Negative Energy

☐ Poor Sleep Quality   ☐ Toxic Overload   ☐ Digital Device Overload

☐ Lack of Movement   ☐ Low Vibe Foods   ☐ Other/ Explain

High Vibe Checklist:

☐ Well Hydrated
☐ No Alcohol
☐ Positive Energy

☐ Great Sleep Quality
☐ Low Toxic Input
☐ Digital Device Balance

☐ Movement
☐ High Vibe Foods
☐ Other/Explain

I will use my creative magic by:

I will move my energy by:

Energy report:

Note from my higher self:

MY
DAILY
VIBE

Vibe I feel right now:

Vibe I want to feel:

5 things I am grateful for:

    1.

    2.

    3.

    4.

    5.

Draw your mood:

Low Vibe Checklist:

☐ Low Water Intake	☐ Alcohol	☐ Negative Energy
☐ Poor Sleep Quality	☐ Toxic Overload	☐ Digital Device Overload
☐ Lack of Movement	☐ Low Vibe Foods	☐ Other/ Explain

High Vibe Checklist:

- ☐ Well Hydrated
- ☐ No Alcohol
- ☐ Positive Energy
- ☐ Great Sleep Quality
- ☐ Low Toxic Input
- ☐ Digital Device Balance
- ☐ Movement
- ☐ High Vibe Foods
- ☐ Other/Explain

I will use my creative magic by:

I will move my energy by:

Energy report:

Note from my higher self:

MY DAILY VIBE

Vibe I feel right now:

Vibe I want to feel:

5 things I am grateful for:

1.

2.

3.

4.

5.

Draw your mood:

Low Vibe Checklist:

☐ Low Water Intake   ☐ Alcohol   ☐ Negative Energy

☐ Poor Sleep Quality   ☐ Toxic Overload   ☐ Digital Device Overload

☐ Lack of Movement   ☐ Low Vibe Foods   ☐ Other/ Explain

High Vibe Checklist:

- [ ] Well Hydrated
- [ ] Great Sleep Quality
- [ ] Movement

- [ ] No Alcohol
- [ ] Low Toxic Input
- [ ] High Vibe Foods

- [ ] Positive Energy
- [ ] Digital Device Balance
- [ ] Other/Explain

I will use my creative magic by:

I will move my energy by:

Energy report:

Note from my higher self:

MY DAILY VIBE

Vibe I feel right now:

Vibe I want to feel:

5 things I am grateful for:

1.

2.

3.

4.

5.

Draw your mood:

Low Vibe Checklist:

☐ Low Water Intake   ☐ Alcohol   ☐ Negative Energy

☐ Poor Sleep Quality   ☐ Toxic Overload   ☐ Digital Device Overload

☐ Lack of Movement   ☐ Low Vibe Foods   ☐ Other/ Explain

High Vibe Checklist:

- [ ] Well Hydrated
- [ ] Great Sleep Quality
- [ ] Movement
- [ ] No Alcohol
- [ ] Low Toxic Input
- [ ] High Vibe Foods
- [ ] Positive Energy
- [ ] Digital Device Balance
- [ ] Other/Explain

I will use my creative magic by:

I will move my energy by:

Energy report:

Note from my higher self:

MY DAILY VIBE

Vibe I feel right now:

Vibe I want to feel:

5 things I am grateful for:

1.

2.

3.

4.

5.

Draw your mood:

Low Vibe Checklist:

☐ Low Water Intake

☐ Alcohol

☐ Negative Energy

☐ Poor Sleep Quality

☐ Toxic Overload

☐ Digital Device Overload

☐ Lack of Movement

☐ Low Vibe Foods

☐ Other/ Explain

High Vibe Checklist:

☐ Well Hydrated   ☐ No Alcohol   ☐ Positive Energy

☐ Great Sleep Quality   ☐ Low Toxic Input   ☐ Digital Device Balance

☐ Movement   ☐ High Vibe Foods   ☐ Other/Explain

I will use my creative magic by:

I will move my energy by:

Energy report:

Note from my higher self:

MY DAILY VIBE

Vibe I feel right now:

Vibe I want to feel:

5 things I am grateful for:

1.

2.

3.

4.

5.

Draw your mood:

Low Vibe Checklist:

☐ Low Water Intake ☐ Alcohol ☐ Negative Energy

☐ Poor Sleep Quality ☐ Toxic Overload ☐ Digital Device Overload

☐ Lack of Movement ☐ Low Vibe Foods ☐ Other/ Explain

High Vibe Checklist:

☐ Well Hydrated   ☐ No Alcohol   ☐ Positive Energy

☐ Great Sleep Quality   ☐ Low Toxic Input   ☐ Digital Device Balance

☐ Movement   ☐ High Vibe Foods   ☐ Other/Explain

I will use my creative magic by:

I will move my energy by:

Energy report:

Note from my higher self:

MY DAILY VIBE

Vibe I feel right now:

Vibe I want to feel:

5 things I am grateful for:

1.

2.

3.

4.

5.

Draw your mood:

Low Vibe Checklist:

☐ Low Water Intake   ☐ Alcohol   ☐ Negative Energy

☐ Poor Sleep Quality   ☐ Toxic Overload   ☐ Digital Device Overload

☐ Lack of Movement   ☐ Low Vibe Foods   ☐ Other/ Explain

High Vibe Checklist:

- ☐ Well Hydrated
- ☐ No Alcohol
- ☐ Positive Energy
- ☐ Great Sleep Quality
- ☐ Low Toxic Input
- ☐ Digital Device Balance
- ☐ Movement
- ☐ High Vibe Foods
- ☐ Other/Explain

I will use my creative magic by:

I will move my energy by:

Energy report:

Note from my higher self:

MY DAILY VIBE

Vibe I feel right now:

Vibe I want to feel:

5 things I am grateful for:

1.

2.

3.

4.

5.

Draw your mood:

Low Vibe Checklist:

☐ Low Water Intake

☐ Alcohol

☐ Negative Energy

☐ Poor Sleep Quality

☐ Toxic Overload

☐ Digital Device Overload

☐ Lack of Movement

☐ Low Vibe Foods

☐ Other/ Explain

High Vibe Checklist:

☐ Well Hydrated   ☐ No Alcohol   ☐ Positive Energy

☐ Great Sleep Quality   ☐ Low Toxic Input   ☐ Digital Device Balance

☐ Movement   ☐ High Vibe Foods   ☐ Other/Explain

I will use my creative magic by:

I will move my energy by:

Energy report:

Note from my higher self:

MY DAILY VIBE

Vibe I feel right now:

Vibe I want to feel:

5 things I am grateful for:

1.

2.

3.

4.

5.

Draw your mood:

Low Vibe Checklist:

☐ Low Water Intake   ☐ Alcohol   ☐ Negative Energy

☐ Poor Sleep Quality   ☐ Toxic Overload   ☐ Digital Device Overload

☐ Lack of Movement   ☐ Low Vibe Foods   ☐ Other/ Explain

High Vibe Checklist:

☐ Well Hydrated   ☐ No Alcohol   ☐ Positive Energy

☐ Great Sleep Quality   ☐ Low Toxic Input   ☐ Digital Device Balance

☐ Movement   ☐ High Vibe Foods   ☐ Other/Explain

I will use my creative magic by:

I will move my energy by:

Energy report:

Note from my higher self:

MY
DAILY
VIBE

Vibe I feel right now:

Vibe I want to feel:

5 things I am grateful for:

    1.

    2.

    3.

    4.

    5.

Draw your mood:

Low Vibe Checklist:

☐ Low Water Intake   ☐ Alcohol   ☐ Negative Energy

☐ Poor Sleep Quality   ☐ Toxic Overload   ☐ Digital Device Overload

☐ Lack of Movement   ☐ Low Vibe Foods   ☐ Other/ Explain

High Vibe Checklist:

- [ ] Well Hydrated
- [ ] Great Sleep Quality
- [ ] Movement

- [ ] No Alcohol
- [ ] Low Toxic Input
- [ ] High Vibe Foods

- [ ] Positive Energy
- [ ] Digital Device Balance
- [ ] Other/Explain

I will use my creative magic by:

I will move my energy by:

Energy report:

Note from my higher self:

MY
DAILY
VIBE

Vibe I feel right now:

Vibe I want to feel:

5 things I am grateful for:

    1.

    2.

    3.

    4.

    5.

Draw your mood:

Low Vibe Checklist:

☐ Low Water Intake	☐ Alcohol	☐ Negative Energy
☐ Poor Sleep Quality	☐ Toxic Overload	☐ Digital Device Overload
☐ Lack of Movement	☐ Low Vibe Foods	☐ Other/ Explain

High Vibe Checklist:

☐ Well Hydrated ☐ No Alcohol ☐ Positive Energy

☐ Great Sleep Quality ☐ Low Toxic Input ☐ Digital Device Balance

☐ Movement ☐ High Vibe Foods ☐ Other/Explain

I will use my creative magic by:

I will move my energy by:

Energy report:

Note from my higher self:

MY DAILY VIBE

Vibe I feel right now:

Vibe I want to feel:

5 things I am grateful for:

1.

2.

3.

4.

5.

Draw your mood:

Low Vibe Checklist:

☐ Low Water Intake   ☐ Alcohol   ☐ Negative Energy

☐ Poor Sleep Quality   ☐ Toxic Overload   ☐ Digital Device Overload

☐ Lack of Movement   ☐ Low Vibe Foods   ☐ Other/ Explain

High Vibe Checklist:

- [ ] Well Hydrated
- [ ] No Alcohol
- [ ] Positive Energy
- [ ] Great Sleep Quality
- [ ] Low Toxic Input
- [ ] Digital Device Balance
- [ ] Movement
- [ ] High Vibe Foods
- [ ] Other/Explain

I will use my creative magic by:

I will move my energy by:

Energy report:

Note from my higher self:

MY DAILY VIBE

Vibe I feel right now:

Vibe I want to feel:

5 things I am grateful for:

    1.

    2.

    3.

    4.

    5.

Draw your mood:

Low Vibe Checklist:

- ☐ Low Water Intake
- ☐ Poor Sleep Quality
- ☐ Lack of Movement
- ☐ Alcohol
- ☐ Toxic Overload
- ☐ Low Vibe Foods
- ☐ Negative Energy
- ☐ Digital Device Overload
- ☐ Other/ Explain

High Vibe Checklist:

☐ Well Hydrated	☐ No Alcohol	☐ Positive Energy
☐ Great Sleep Quality	☐ Low Toxic Input	☐ Digital Device Balance
☐ Movement	☐ High Vibe Foods	☐ Other/Explain

I will use my creative magic by:

I will move my energy by:

Energy report:

Note from my higher self:

MY
DAILY
VIBE

Vibe I feel right now:

Vibe I want to feel:

5 things I am grateful for:

    1.

    2.

    3.

    4.

    5.

Draw your mood:

Low Vibe Checklist:

☐ Low Water Intake   ☐ Alcohol   ☐ Negative Energy

☐ Poor Sleep Quality   ☐ Toxic Overload   ☐ Digital Device Overload

☐ Lack of Movement   ☐ Low Vibe Foods   ☐ Other/ Explain

High Vibe Checklist:

☐ Well Hydrated ☐ No Alcohol ☐ Positive Energy

☐ Great Sleep Quality ☐ Low Toxic Input ☐ Digital Device Balance

☐ Movement ☐ High Vibe Foods ☐ Other/Explain

I will use my creative magic by:

I will move my energy by:

Energy report:

Note from my higher self:

MY DAILY VIBE

Vibe I feel right now:

Vibe I want to feel:

5 things I am grateful for:

1.

2.

3.

4.

5.

Draw your mood:

Low Vibe Checklist:

☐ Low Water Intake   ☐ Alcohol   ☐ Negative Energy

☐ Poor Sleep Quality   ☐ Toxic Overload   ☐ Digital Device Overload

☐ Lack of Movement   ☐ Low Vibe Foods   ☐ Other/ Explain

High Vibe Checklist:

☐ Well Hydrated   ☐ No Alcohol   ☐ Positive Energy

☐ Great Sleep Quality   ☐ Low Toxic Input   ☐ Digital Device Balance

☐ Movement   ☐ High Vibe Foods   ☐ Other/Explain

I will use my creative magic by:

I will move my energy by:

Energy report:

Note from my higher self:

MY
DAILY
VIBE

Vibe I feel right now:

Vibe I want to feel:

5 things I am grateful for:

    1.

    2.

    3.

    4.

    5.

Draw your mood:

Low Vibe Checklist:

☐ Low Water Intake	☐ Alcohol	☐ Negative Energy
☐ Poor Sleep Quality	☐ Toxic Overload	☐ Digital Device Overload
☐ Lack of Movement	☐ Low Vibe Foods	☐ Other/ Explain

High Vibe Checklist:

☐ Well Hydrated   ☐ No Alcohol   ☐ Positive Energy

☐ Great Sleep Quality   ☐ Low Toxic Input   ☐ Digital Device Balance

☐ Movement   ☐ High Vibe Foods   ☐ Other/Explain

I will use my creative magic by:

I will move my energy by:

Energy report:

Note from my higher self:

MY DAILY VIBE

Vibe I feel right now:

Vibe I want to feel:

5 things I am grateful for:

1.

2.

3.

4.

5.

Draw your mood:

Low Vibe Checklist:

☐ Low Water Intake   ☐ Alcohol   ☐ Negative Energy

☐ Poor Sleep Quality   ☐ Toxic Overload   ☐ Digital Device Overload

☐ Lack of Movement   ☐ Low Vibe Foods   ☐ Other/ Explain

High Vibe Checklist:

☐ Well Hydrated   ☐ No Alcohol   ☐ Positive Energy

☐ Great Sleep Quality   ☐ Low Toxic Input   ☐ Digital Device Balance

☐ Movement   ☐ High Vibe Foods   ☐ Other/Explain

I will use my creative magic by:

I will move my energy by:

Energy report:

Note from my higher self:

MY DAILY VIBE

Vibe I feel right now:

Vibe I want to feel:

5 things I am grateful for:

    1.

    2.

    3.

    4.

    5.

Draw your mood:

Low Vibe Checklist:

☐ Low Water Intake   ☐ Alcohol   ☐ Negative Energy

☐ Poor Sleep Quality   ☐ Toxic Overload   ☐ Digital Device Overload

☐ Lack of Movement   ☐ Low Vibe Foods   ☐ Other/ Explain

High Vibe Checklist:

☐ Well Hydrated   ☐ No Alcohol   ☐ Positive Energy

☐ Great Sleep Quality   ☐ Low Toxic Input   ☐ Digital Device Balance

☐ Movement   ☐ High Vibe Foods   ☐ Other/Explain

I will use my creative magic by:

I will move my energy by:

Energy report:

Note from my higher self:

MY DAILY VIBE

Vibe I feel right now:

Vibe I want to feel:

5 things I am grateful for:

    1.

    2.

    3.

    4.

    5.

Draw your mood:

Low Vibe Checklist:

☐ Low Water Intake	☐ Alcohol	☐ Negative Energy
☐ Poor Sleep Quality	☐ Toxic Overload	☐ Digital Device Overload
☐ Lack of Movement	☐ Low Vibe Foods	☐ Other/ Explain

High Vibe Checklist:

☐ Well Hydrated ☐ No Alcohol ☐ Positive Energy

☐ Great Sleep Quality ☐ Low Toxic Input ☐ Digital Device Balance

☐ Movement ☐ High Vibe Foods ☐ Other/Explain

I will use my creative magic by:

I will move my energy by:

Energy report:

Note from my higher self:

MY
DAILY
VIBE

Vibe I feel right now:

Vibe I want to feel:

5 things I am grateful for:

    1.

    2.

    3.

    4.

    5.

Draw your mood:

Low Vibe Checklist:

☐ Low Water Intake   ☐ Alcohol   ☐ Negative Energy

☐ Poor Sleep Quality   ☐ Toxic Overload   ☐ Digital Device Overload

☐ Lack of Movement   ☐ Low Vibe Foods   ☐ Other/ Explain

High Vibe Checklist:

- ☐ Well Hydrated
- ☐ No Alcohol
- ☐ Positive Energy
- ☐ Great Sleep Quality
- ☐ Low Toxic Input
- ☐ Digital Device Balance
- ☐ Movement
- ☐ High Vibe Foods
- ☐ Other/Explain

🌈 I will use my creative magic by:

♂ I will move my energy by:

⚡ Energy report:

🪷 Note from my higher self:

MY DAILY VIBE

Vibe I feel right now:

Vibe I want to feel:

5 things I am grateful for:

1.

2.

3.

4.

5.

Draw your mood:

Low Vibe Checklist:

☐ Low Water Intake   ☐ Alcohol   ☐ Negative Energy

☐ Poor Sleep Quality   ☐ Toxic Overload   ☐ Digital Device Overload

☐ Lack of Movement   ☐ Low Vibe Foods   ☐ Other/ Explain

High Vibe Checklist:

☐ Well Hydrated ☐ No Alcohol ☐ Positive Energy

☐ Great Sleep Quality ☐ Low Toxic Input ☐ Digital Device Balance

☐ Movement ☐ High Vibe Foods ☐ Other/Explain

I will use my creative magic by:

I will move my energy by:

Energy report:

Note from my higher self:

MY
DAILY
VIBE

Vibe I feel right now:

Vibe I want to feel:

5 things I am grateful for:

1.

2.

3.

4.

5.

Draw your mood:

Low Vibe Checklist:

☐ Low Water Intake   ☐ Alcohol   ☐ Negative Energy

☐ Poor Sleep Quality   ☐ Toxic Overload   ☐ Digital Device Overload

☐ Lack of Movement   ☐ Low Vibe Foods   ☐ Other/ Explain

High Vibe Checklist:

☐ Well Hydrated   ☐ No Alcohol   ☐ Positive Energy

☐ Great Sleep Quality   ☐ Low Toxic Input   ☐ Digital Device Balance

☐ Movement   ☐ High Vibe Foods   ☐ Other/Explain

I will use my creative magic by:

I will move my energy by:

Energy report:

Note from my higher self:

MY DAILY VIBE

Vibe I feel right now:

Vibe I want to feel:

5 things I am grateful for:

    1.

    2.

    3.

    4.

    5.

Draw your mood:

Low Vibe Checklist:

☐ Low Water Intake   ☐ Alcohol   ☐ Negative Energy

☐ Poor Sleep Quality   ☐ Toxic Overload   ☐ Digital Device Overload

☐ Lack of Movement   ☐ Low Vibe Foods   ☐ Other/ Explain

High Vibe Checklist:

- ☐ Well Hydrated
- ☐ Great Sleep Quality
- ☐ Movement

- ☐ No Alcohol
- ☐ Low Toxic Input
- ☐ High Vibe Foods

- ☐ Positive Energy
- ☐ Digital Device Balance
- ☐ Other/Explain

I will use my creative magic by:

I will move my energy by:

Energy report:

Note from my higher self:

MY DAILY VIBE

Vibe I feel right now:

Vibe I want to feel:

5 things I am grateful for:

1.

2.

3.

4.

5.

Draw your mood:

Low Vibe Checklist:

☐ Low Water Intake	☐ Alcohol	☐ Negative Energy
☐ Poor Sleep Quality	☐ Toxic Overload	☐ Digital Device Overload
☐ Lack of Movement	☐ Low Vibe Foods	☐ Other/ Explain

High Vibe Checklist:

☐ Well Hydrated ☐ No Alcohol ☐ Positive Energy

☐ Great Sleep Quality ☐ Low Toxic Input ☐ Digital Device Balance

☐ Movement ☐ High Vibe Foods ☐ Other/Explain

I will use my creative magic by:

I will move my energy by:

Energy report:

Note from my higher self:

MY DAILY VIBE

Vibe I feel right now:

Vibe I want to feel:

5 things I am grateful for:

1.

2.

3.

4.

5.

Draw your mood:

Low Vibe Checklist:

☐ Low Water Intake   ☐ Alcohol   ☐ Negative Energy

☐ Poor Sleep Quality   ☐ Toxic Overload   ☐ Digital Device Overload

☐ Lack of Movement   ☐ Low Vibe Foods   ☐ Other/ Explain

High Vibe Checklist:

- ☐ Well Hydrated
- ☐ No Alcohol
- ☐ Positive Energy
- ☐ Great Sleep Quality
- ☐ Low Toxic Input
- ☐ Digital Device Balance
- ☐ Movement
- ☐ High Vibe Foods
- ☐ Other/Explain

I will use my creative magic by:

I will move my energy by:

Energy report:

Note from my higher self:

MY DAILY VIBE

Vibe I feel right now:

Vibe I want to feel:

5 things I am grateful for:

    1.

    2.

    3.

    4.

    5.

Draw your mood:

Low Vibe Checklist:

☐ Low Water Intake	☐ Alcohol	☐ Negative Energy
☐ Poor Sleep Quality	☐ Toxic Overload	☐ Digital Device Overload
☐ Lack of Movement	☐ Low Vibe Foods	☐ Other/ Explain

High Vibe Checklist:

☐ Well Hydrated

☐ No Alcohol

☐ Positive Energy

☐ Great Sleep Quality

☐ Low Toxic Input

☐ Digital Device Balance

☐ Movement

☐ High Vibe Foods

☐ Other/Explain

I will use my creative magic by:

I will move my energy by:

Energy report:

Note from my higher self:

MY
DAILY
VIBE

Vibe I feel right now:

Vibe I want to feel:

5 things I am grateful for:

1.

2.

3.

4.

5.

Draw your mood:

Low Vibe Checklist:

☐ Low Water Intake   ☐ Alcohol   ☐ Negative Energy

☐ Poor Sleep Quality   ☐ Toxic Overload   ☐ Digital Device Overload

☐ Lack of Movement   ☐ Low Vibe Foods   ☐ Other/ Explain

High Vibe Checklist:

- [ ] Well Hydrated
- [ ] No Alcohol
- [ ] Positive Energy
- [ ] Great Sleep Quality
- [ ] Low Toxic Input
- [ ] Digital Device Balance
- [ ] Movement
- [ ] High Vibe Foods
- [ ] Other/Explain

I will use my creative magic by:

I will move my energy by:

Energy report:

Note from my higher self:

MY DAILY VIBE

Vibe I feel right now:

Vibe I want to feel:

5 things I am grateful for:

1.

2.

3.

4.

5.

Draw your mood:

Low Vibe Checklist:

☐ Low Water Intake ☐ Alcohol ☐ Negative Energy

☐ Poor Sleep Quality ☐ Toxic Overload ☐ Digital Device Overload

☐ Lack of Movement ☐ Low Vibe Foods ☐ Other/ Explain

High Vibe Checklist:

- ☐ Well Hydrated
- ☐ Great Sleep Quality
- ☐ Movement
- ☐ No Alcohol
- ☐ Low Toxic Input
- ☐ High Vibe Foods
- ☐ Positive Energy
- ☐ Digital Device Balance
- ☐ Other/Explain

I will use my creative magic by:

I will move my energy by:

Energy report:

Note from my higher self:

MY DAILY VIBE

Vibe I feel right now:

Vibe I want to feel:

5 things I am grateful for:

1.

2.

3.

4.

5.

Draw your mood:

Low Vibe Checklist:

☐ Low Water Intake   ☐ Alcohol   ☐ Negative Energy

☐ Poor Sleep Quality   ☐ Toxic Overload   ☐ Digital Device Overload

☐ Lack of Movement   ☐ Low Vibe Foods   ☐ Other/ Explain

High Vibe Checklist:

☐ Well Hydrated
☐ No Alcohol
☐ Positive Energy

☐ Great Sleep Quality
☐ Low Toxic Input
☐ Digital Device Balance

☐ Movement
☐ High Vibe Foods
☐ Other/Explain

I will use my creative magic by:

I will move my energy by:

Energy report:

Note from my higher self:

MY DAILY VIBE

Vibe I feel right now:

Vibe I want to feel:

5 things I am grateful for:

1.

2.

3.

4.

5.

Draw your mood:

Low Vibe Checklist:

☐ Low Water Intake   ☐ Alcohol   ☐ Negative Energy

☐ Poor Sleep Quality   ☐ Toxic Overload   ☐ Digital Device Overload

☐ Lack of Movement   ☐ Low Vibe Foods   ☐ Other/ Explain

High Vibe Checklist:

☐ Well Hydrated ☐ No Alcohol ☐ Positive Energy

☐ Great Sleep Quality ☐ Low Toxic Input ☐ Digital Device Balance

☐ Movement ☐ High Vibe Foods ☐ Other/Explain

I will use my creative magic by:

I will move my energy by:

Energy report:

Note from my higher self:

MY DAILY VIBE

Vibe I feel right now:

Vibe I want to feel:

5 things I am grateful for:

1.

2.

3.

4.

5.

Draw your mood:

Low Vibe Checklist:

☐ Low Water Intake

☐ Alcohol

☐ Negative Energy

☐ Poor Sleep Quality

☐ Toxic Overload

☐ Digital Device Overload

☐ Lack of Movement

☐ Low Vibe Foods

☐ Other/ Explain

High Vibe Checklist:

- [ ] Well Hydrated
- [ ] No Alcohol
- [ ] Positive Energy
- [ ] Great Sleep Quality
- [ ] Low Toxic Input
- [ ] Digital Device Balance
- [ ] Movement
- [ ] High Vibe Foods
- [ ] Other/Explain

I will use my creative magic by:

I will move my energy by:

Energy report:

Note from my higher self:

MY DAILY VIBE

Vibe I feel right now:

Vibe I want to feel:

5 things I am grateful for:

1.

2.

3.

4.

5.

Draw your mood:

Low Vibe Checklist:

☐ Low Water Intake

☐ Alcohol

☐ Negative Energy

☐ Poor Sleep Quality

☐ Toxic Overload

☐ Digital Device Overload

☐ Lack of Movement

☐ Low Vibe Foods

☐ Other/ Explain

High Vibe Checklist:

☐ Well Hydrated ☐ No Alcohol ☐ Positive Energy

☐ Great Sleep Quality ☐ Low Toxic Input ☐ Digital Device Balance

☐ Movement ☐ High Vibe Foods ☐ Other/Explain

I will use my creative magic by:

I will move my energy by:

Energy report:

Note from my higher self:

MY DAILY VIBE

Vibe I feel right now:

Vibe I want to feel:

5 things I am grateful for:

1.

2.

3.

4.

5.

Draw your mood:

Low Vibe Checklist:

☐ Low Water Intake   ☐ Alcohol   ☐ Negative Energy

☐ Poor Sleep Quality   ☐ Toxic Overload   ☐ Digital Device Overload

☐ Lack of Movement   ☐ Low Vibe Foods   ☐ Other/ Explain

High Vibe Checklist:

☐ Well Hydrated ☐ No Alcohol ☐ Positive Energy

☐ Great Sleep Quality ☐ Low Toxic Input ☐ Digital Device Balance

☐ Movement ☐ High Vibe Foods ☐ Other/Explain

I will use my creative magic by:

I will move my energy by:

Energy report:

Note from my higher self:

MY DAILY VIBE

Vibe I feel right now:

Vibe I want to feel:

5 things I am grateful for:

1.

2.

3.

4.

5.

Draw your mood:

Low Vibe Checklist:

☐ Low Water Intake

☐ Poor Sleep Quality

☐ Lack of Movement

☐ Alcohol

☐ Toxic Overload

☐ Low Vibe Foods

☐ Negative Energy

☐ Digital Device Overload

☐ Other/ Explain

High Vibe Checklist:

- ☐ Well Hydrated
- ☐ No Alcohol
- ☐ Positive Energy
- ☐ Great Sleep Quality
- ☐ Low Toxic Input
- ☐ Digital Device Balance
- ☐ Movement
- ☐ High Vibe Foods
- ☐ Other/Explain

I will use my creative magic by:

I will move my energy by:

Energy report:

Note from my higher self:

MY DAILY VIBE

Vibe I feel right now:

Vibe I want to feel:

5 things I am grateful for:

    1.

    2.

    3.

    4.

    5.

Draw your mood:

Low Vibe Checklist:

☐ Low Water Intake	☐ Alcohol	☐ Negative Energy
☐ Poor Sleep Quality	☐ Toxic Overload	☐ Digital Device Overload
☐ Lack of Movement	☐ Low Vibe Foods	☐ Other/ Explain

High Vibe Checklist:

☐ Well Hydrated ☐ No Alcohol ☐ Positive Energy

☐ Great Sleep Quality ☐ Low Toxic Input ☐ Digital Device Balance

☐ Movement ☐ High Vibe Foods ☐ Other/Explain

I will use my creative magic by:

I will move my energy by:

Energy report:

Note from my higher self:

MY DAILY VIBE

Vibe I feel right now:

Vibe I want to feel:

5 things I am grateful for:

1.

2.

3.

4.

5.

Draw your mood:

Low Vibe Checklist:

☐ Low Water Intake

☐ Alcohol

☐ Negative Energy

☐ Poor Sleep Quality

☐ Toxic Overload

☐ Digital Device Overload

☐ Lack of Movement

☐ Low Vibe Foods

☐ Other/ Explain

High Vibe Checklist:

☐ Well
Hydrated

☐ No
Alcohol

☐ Positive
Energy

☐ Great Sleep
Quality

☐ Low Toxic
Input

☐ Digital Device
Balance

☐ Movement

☐ High Vibe
Foods

☐ Other/Explain

I will use my creative magic by:

I will move my energy by:

Energy report:

Note from my higher self:

MY DAILY VIBE

Vibe I feel right now:

Vibe I want to feel:

5 things I am grateful for:

    1.

    2.

    3.

    4.

    5.

Draw your mood:

Low Vibe Checklist:

- ☐ Low Water Intake
- ☐ Alcohol
- ☐ Negative Energy
- ☐ Poor Sleep Quality
- ☐ Toxic Overload
- ☐ Digital Device Overload
- ☐ Lack of Movement
- ☐ Low Vibe Foods
- ☐ Other/ Explain

High Vibe Checklist:

- ☐ Well Hydrated
- ☐ Great Sleep Quality
- ☐ Movement

- ☐ No Alcohol
- ☐ Low Toxic Input
- ☐ High Vibe Foods

- ☐ Positive Energy
- ☐ Digital Device Balance
- ☐ Other/Explain

I will use my creative magic by:

I will move my energy by:

Energy report:

Note from my higher self:

MY DAILY VIBE

Vibe I feel right now:

Vibe I want to feel:

5 things I am grateful for:

    1.

    2.

    3.

    4.

    5.

Draw your mood:

Low Vibe Checklist:

☐ Low Water Intake	☐ Alcohol	☐ Negative Energy
☐ Poor Sleep Quality	☐ Toxic Overload	☐ Digital Device Overload
☐ Lack of Movement	☐ Low Vibe Foods	☐ Other/ Explain

High Vibe Checklist:

- [ ] Well Hydrated
- [ ] Great Sleep Quality
- [ ] Movement
- [ ] No Alcohol
- [ ] Low Toxic Input
- [ ] High Vibe Foods
- [ ] Positive Energy
- [ ] Digital Device Balance
- [ ] Other/Explain

I will use my creative magic by:

I will move my energy by:

Energy report:

Note from my higher self:

MY
DAILY
VIBE

Vibe I feel right now:

Vibe I want to feel:

5 things I am grateful for:

    1.

    2.

    3.

    4.

    5.

Draw your mood:

Low Vibe Checklist:

☐ Low Water Intake   ☐ Alcohol   ☐ Negative Energy

☐ Poor Sleep Quality   ☐ Toxic Overload   ☐ Digital Device Overload

☐ Lack of Movement   ☐ Low Vibe Foods   ☐ Other/ Explain

High Vibe Checklist:

☐ Well Hydrated   ☐ No Alcohol   ☐ Positive Energy

☐ Great Sleep Quality   ☐ Low Toxic Input   ☐ Digital Device Balance

☐ Movement   ☐ High Vibe Foods   ☐ Other/Explain

I will use my creative magic by:

I will move my energy by:

Energy report:

Note from my higher self:

MY DAILY VIBE

Vibe I feel right now:

Vibe I want to feel:

5 things I am grateful for:

1.

2.

3.

4.

5.

Draw your mood:

Low Vibe Checklist:

☐ Low Water
Intake

☐ Alcohol

☐ Negative
Energy

☐ Poor Sleep
Quality

☐ Toxic
Overload

☐ Digital Device
Overload

☐ Lack of
Movement

☐ Low Vibe
Foods

☐ Other/
Explain

High Vibe Checklist:

☐ Well Hydrated   ☐ No Alcohol   ☐ Positive Energy

☐ Great Sleep Quality   ☐ Low Toxic Input   ☐ Digital Device Balance

☐ Movement   ☐ High Vibe Foods   ☐ Other/Explain

I will use my creative magic by:

I will move my energy by:

Energy report:

Note from my higher self:

MY DAILY VIBE

Vibe I feel right now:

Vibe I want to feel:

5 things I am grateful for:

    1.

    2.

    3.

    4.

    5.

Draw your mood:

Low Vibe Checklist:

☐ Low Water Intake	☐ Alcohol	☐ Negative Energy
☐ Poor Sleep Quality	☐ Toxic Overload	☐ Digital Device Overload
☐ Lack of Movement	☐ Low Vibe Foods	☐ Other/ Explain

High Vibe Checklist:

- ☐ Well Hydrated
- ☐ Great Sleep Quality
- ☐ Movement
- ☐ No Alcohol
- ☐ Low Toxic Input
- ☐ High Vibe Foods
- ☐ Positive Energy
- ☐ Digital Device Balance
- ☐ Other/Explain

I will use my creative magic by:

I will move my energy by:

Energy report:

Note from my higher self:

CPSIA information can be obtained
at www.ICGtesting.com
Printed in the USA
BVHW041633040222
627987BV00014B/611